COME-BY-CHANCE

a collection of poems

CARL LEGGO

Breakwater Books Ltd.
100 Water Street • P.O. Box 2188 • St. John's • NL • A1C 6E6
www.breakwaterbooks.com

Library and Archives Canada Cataloguing in Publication

Leggo, Carleton Derek, 1953-

Come-By-Chance / Carl Leggo.

Poems.

ISBN 1-55081-082-0

I. Title.

PS8573.E461725C65 2006 C811'.54 C2006-903898-8

Editor: Tom Henihan
Cover Photography: Ray Fennelly
Artwork held at the Collection of Memorial University of Newfoundland

The Canada Council for the Arts | Le Conseil des Arts du Canada

We acknowledge the financial support of The Canada Council for the Arts for our publishing activities.

We acknowledge the support of the Department of Tourism, Culture and Recreation for our publishing activities.

Canadä

We acknowledge the financial support of the Government of Canada through the Book Publishing Industry Development Program (BPIDP) for our publishing activities.

Printed in Canada.

For Lana who fills my life with her heart's light,
and for her parents, Chesley and Vivian,
and her sisters, Lynda, Lorna, and Joanne,
who know together the source of light in love.

TABLE OF CONTENTS

WEST COAST PRAIRIE

Last Saturday, biking the dike around Lulu Island, a sweeping sand sculpture in the mouth of the Fraser River, Norm asked why I had moved to Richmond, and I confessed

economic necessity, and Norm said he chose Richmond because it is flat and has farms like Saskatchewan, and how when he first moved here, years ago, the Coast Mountains

around English Bay held only threats, the world written in the geography of our growing up, and I told him about Corner Brook curled in the Humber Arm, the world's biggest

paper mill belching sulphite steam smoke ceaselessly, except Christmas and Labour Day, and how I always thought the world had come to Corner Brook with Hollywood,

Eaton's catalogues, and visits by famous people like Pierre and Margaret Trudeau, Gordon Lightfoot, Ian and Sylvia, Gordie Howe and the Queen, until at 15,

I visited Montreal and couldn't believe how big the world was, and after growing up perpendicular on the side of a hill like a robust Merlot kissed by wild autumn,

spring ice, summer heat, and winter light with long shadows on the retina of the heart, I now live in Richmond's long wet season, flat like Saskatchewan, reminiscing about

Jigg's dinner, dark rum, cod tongues, stewed moose, fish and brewis, Celtic rhythms, Al Pittman's poetry, Skipper's rants, *Stripping the Willow* with Eddy Ezekiel on accordion, always going back in my poems, knowing that I never really left, knowing that we can never really go back to the world written in the geography of our growing up.

§ § §

COME-BY-CHANCE

From Corner Brook, I drive the Trans-Canada
across Newfoundland on a bare black highway
under a blue March sky.

I am surprised how little has changed,
how well I remember the land's writing.

The sun falls as I drive through the late afternoon:
I chant with the sun's ancient blood rhythms.

In an ESSO overlooking Random Sound
I eat fish cakes and later drink a Black Horse
at the Tanker Inn near Come-By-Chance.

The whole world is at rest like anything could happen,
like nothing's going to happen,

perhaps the world has simply stopped on a Wednesday night
in this vast vacant island where an eternal flame

burns in the night sky over a moth-balled oil refinery,
a steady sign that Joey Smallwood had less sense and more dreams
than a narcoleptic on valium.

Having nothing else to do, we watch CBC with gulls' weary eyes,
another documentary on Barbara Ann Scott,
still skating with a frozen smile,

and Mel tells me the roads are slippery and complains about politicians
who won't provide enough salt trucks for the highway.

I nod.

RHIZOME

Newfoundland is far away and Lynch's Lane lingers in imagination
and poetry, but last night my mother called with more stories:

Cindy Mercer, my third or fourth cousin perhaps,
but definitely a Mercer like my grandmother and mother,
met a man through the Internet, moved to Australia and married him.

Cindy Mercer's father said: "Nice as you could meet anywhere,"
as if there was some doubt, some need to defend Australian niceness.

And one April morning with a muffled breath of spring,
Sal Mercer, who never spent a cent,
hiked the Heights to the new Wal-Mart
and collapsed as the automatic doors opened,

nine decades of stories gone before the ambulance arrived,
though there are Mercers everywhere

    married in Australia
    on their way to Wal-Mart
    seeking poems in British Columbia

like holograms, the part in the whole, rhizome connections in the earth,
the sheer certitude of lives spelling out in fractal inevitability.

§ § §

SEVEN SPARROWS

Sipping a rye and seven
on Nan and Pop's patio, I see
seven yellow-backed sparrows
light in the lime tips of a spruce

like ceramic miniatures from Red Rose tea,
small enough to be almost real,
they peck at the branches, feast on budworms,
while crows watch from telephone lines.

I remember my daughter brought the spruce home
from S.D. Cook Elementary,
a seedling in a Dixie cup on Save the Earth Day,
and because we were in transit for a year

from Alberta to British Columbia
and home again to Newfoundland,
Pop planted it in his backyard and for years
feared he mowed the spruce with the daisies,

and now it holds sparrows, the longing of crows,
and memories enough to keep the heart calling
earth's rhythms with roots seeking deep and deeper,
the whole earth sung in veins of long light.

RAISIN BREAD

Down Lynch's Lane in the winter's night, Cec's mother Sue carried in a tea towel, loaves of raisin molasses bread just out of the oven, margarine glistening like street lights on midnight snow. When we broke the bread's crisp skin, steam rose and warmed all Lynch's Lane and as we ate we all agreed that Sue made the world's best bread, conjuring memories of tropical places we'd never seen.

Francis Dove worked as a cook at the Glynmill Inn, boarded with Hazel Gullage and fell in love with her daughter Winnie, who was years older than him. When Hazel died, Francis's mother moved in and because the two women were difficult to tell apart, we called them Francis Dove's women and dreamed of having a harem like the sultan of Brunei.

For thirty-three years, Eli Cunningham worked for Lundrigan's Construction and looked forward to a pension and a house trailer in Florida. However, nineteen months before his pension eligibility, Lundrigan's laid Eli off with a brass barometer, which pointed to high pressure and no pension. But as luck would have it, Eli didn't really need a pension as he died of a heart attack a few months later.

Mrs. Jennings lived in the best house on Lynch's Lane with a short-cropped lawn, a border of tall alders and fruit trees in the backyard. On Tuesdays, Sue sometimes said, "Mrs. Jennings has baked one of her lovely chocolate cakes," and she and Carrie would visit in mid-afternoon, sipping tea like neighbours in *Another World.*

The Weston brothers were always in court over the lines of fences that no one surveyed, land just squatted and claimed in the early 1900's, and Skipper said, "Nothing can destroy a family like a few inches of land, slivers of earth through the heart."

Carrie asked Mamie Gill's daughter, "How is your mother?" Mamie Gill's daughter replied, "She was a hundred years old last week and she's drowning in trivia." Carrie said, "I guess after a century, it's hard not to."

Uncle Sam, always glad for any invitation, crouched in the dark with Pride Weston and her crowd waiting for Gil, who was always contrary as a goose, even on his birthday. Gil Weston saw Uncle Sam in the corner with Pride and barked, "Surprise, I'll give you a surprise." He then yanked the tablecloth from the table, not fast enough to leave everything on the table like on the *Ed Sullivan Show*, but slow enough for chocolate cake, egg sandwiches and raspberry syrup to fill the air. In the dark Uncle Sam walked home, "Not even a drink," he said, "and a week getting egg salad out of my hair."

Late June, the sun almost tucked into the Humber Arm, I walked Dove's Road in my first tweed jacket with Bonnie Lee and Stephanie, with echoes of sky and sea and Bonnie Lee's eyes. I was Rock Hudson in Monaco thinking Bonnie Lee had to be thinking about me in my new jacket, when a hand like a lion's jaw locked my arm and twisted me into the night eyes of Mickey Greening, all snarls and sour breath. Fighting lions was tougher than Tarzan made it seem and I limped home, my jacket a tattered coat of blues and the sky was tar with laughter everywhere, Mickey Greening's, Stephanie's, Bonnie Lee's even, in the evening sky.

For weeks I lifted weights in the basement and punched a painted jute sack stuffed with winter coats, an effigy of Mickey Greening. However, Mickey was caught breaking into Carter's Store and sent to the Whitbourne Reformatory for Juvenile Delinquents. A few years later, Mickey Greening returned to Lynch's Lane praising Jesus with sprays of spit through the few teeth that hadn't been knocked out.

Junie Sweetland, my first love, kindergarten 1958, ran off with Eric when he returned single and still handsome for the 25th high school reunion. A lot of people thought about running away after the reunion, but Junie, who married and had kids after high school, worked in a bookstore and went nowhere, only she, like she was waiting for rescue, ran away after the reunion.

Carrie baked bread at least once a week, and the bread was always charred on the bottom. Carrie always said, "This is the way Skipper likes it." Skipper always said, "This is some good bread."

§ § §

SCRATCH IN MY THROAT

Four black birds sit on the fence
in the snow in my backyard.
This is rare, as it seldom snows in Steveston,
and for a breath I am in Newfoundland

where I lived a long story of winter light
where snow insists on staying too long
in a sacred, sometimes scary land.
The birds remind me of Wallace Stevens

and wondering where the other nine are,
I feel so close to a poem, its breath
a scratch in my throat in the tangled
mist of memories. I live with the past

trailing like a train of U-Hauls stuffed
with stories I no longer need. It is always hard
to clean the closet, especially in winter
when the stories, like old sweaters,

might still be missed, though this morning,
while running on the dike, I heard thousands
of snow geese write their way into the dawn
with a raucous eagerness for light.

SHEEP

Another August, almost forty years ago, I came for the first time to Robinson's, to Buller Evans' Brown Jug Cabins. Standing on this beach today, little changed, I can see the part Australian sheep dog, Tip, still chasing sheep into the ocean. Though he had never seen sheep before he was confident that he knew what to do. Knowing nothing about sheep and the dogs that chase them, I dashed to my parents with a piercing yell, "Tip chased the sheep into the ocean." And in the spirit of accurate news reporting, or a fledgling flourish of poetic fervour, I added, "You can just see the heads of the sheep bobbing on the horizon like a line of ducks." My parents burst into laughter and I laughed, relieved that I didn't have to worry, knowing my parents wouldn't be laughing if there was anything to be concerned about. Eventually, Tip returned and the sheep also, I think. My father gave Buller Evans a bottle of Old Sam and everybody drank at the picnic table telling stories of sheep and sheep dogs and swimming in the wide wild ocean, swollen with the full moon's memories of lunatic longing.

DIZZY DOUCETTE

When tying flies,
Skipper conjures creatures
out of nylon and down,
dyed in countless colours,
flies that look real enough
in late May or June
to trick trout after a lean winter

and he reminisces about Dizzy Doucette,
who drank all the time,
and the winter night Dizzy,
wrapped in his wife's mink stole
to ward off a January blizzard,
sneaked into the Caribou Tavern,
and hid under the ledge of the bar.
Since Pixie Pollett refused to serve him,
Dizzy whispered,
"Skipper, order two beers."
Always glad to be helpful,
Skipper held up two fingers
full of hope for peace,
but Pixie Pollett smiled,
"You can have one, Skipper,
but Dizzie Doucette
is going home sober tonight,"

and when Skipper laments,
“There are no characters any more,”
I want to remind him the characters
are just waiting to be conjured.

SCRIBBLED IN WINTER LIGHT

1

When Margie Kelloway told her husband she was going to learn to ski at Marble Mountain, Cal agreed that physical exercise was just what Margie needed. Margie wasn't getting fat, but she wasn't the Margie he had married. However, after three children in quick succession, Cal Kelloway understood the few extra pounds. Margie learned to ski the black diamond runs. Her ski instructor, Jake Dicks, said she was one of the best students he'd ever taught. Margie was pleased and ordered a new ski suit, red and purple like a winter sunset, from Simpson-Sears. She was a Pentecostal tongue of fire on the ski hills, and Jake Dicks was swept up in passion like a snowball falling down the mountain. When Jake told Margie he loved her, Margie told Cal. Cal swore about how the fellows in the mill always said Marble Mountain was another Peyton Place: "Everybody after everybody they shouldn't be after." Cal drove fast along the Humber River to Steady Brook, found Jake and cracked Jake's skis in splinters. "Next time I'll break your legs," Cal said with a James Cagney growl. That night he took Margie to the Wine Cellar and remembered to tell her how beautiful she was.

2

After a semester at Memorial, I returned home with Lana in December, eager to introduce her to my family. They knew Lana from my letters but this was their first opportunity to meet her. Lana and I almost needed snowshoes to tramp through the deep snow from Eddy's Bus depot up Old Humber Road. When I introduced Lana to my brother, he just nodded and smiled. I knew my brother was shy but I expected a little more effort in his greeting … a story, a question, a little wit. Instead, my brother said nothing, just quickly slipped on his coat and left the house. My brother was a puzzle but Skipper compensated for him with an almost manic burst of stories, jokes and opinions. When it was time for Lana to catch her bus back to Stephenville, we stepped outside to see my brother leaning on a snow shovel with a wide grin. Like Charlton Heston opening the Red Sea, he had shovelled a wide path through the deep snow in the yard. He still didn't say anything, but Lana kissed his hot face as she passed.

LOOKOUT

(for Anna)

Like stars in York Harbour snow,
I have memories of you,
beyond all counting,
beyond all alphabets and words.

No book, no library even,
could hold all the adventures
you have already lived, all written
in the language of the heart's delight.

In one of my favourite photos,
a sliver of the past seized in light,
you are a joyous toddler
strapped securely to my back.

I took the photograph
holding the camera at arm's length
as we hiked a mountain to
Joey's Lookout for a picnic.

In the photo, our round laughing faces
fill the square of caught light.
We look glad we climbed a steep trail,
glad to be together sharing another adventure.
Standing in the centre of a circle of sky, ocean,
forest and mountains that claim our hearts, I
remember I was proud of you, my little daughter,
with your insatiable desire for the heart's delights.

But now, when I search
for that photo I can't find it,
it too has become a sliver of the past
holding the good stories tight.

HOMEWORK

When my son was young,
most nights I helped him
with his homework
and remembered how
Skipper sat close beside me
on the edge of his big bed
while I memorized textbooks
and answered questions.
In spite of long days
in the mill and frequent calls
from neighbours to fix their
ovens, toasters, electric kettles,
Skipper always quizzed me
for tests, sometimes for hours,
and never complained.
When we studied
geography, Skipper said,
"Wherever you go, know
where you come from so
you can find your way back."

MARY MAXIM SWEATER

In a winter blast in March, Skipper went to the Majestic with Carrie. "I couldn't see the movie," he said, "I couldn't see anything because the woman in the seat ahead of me was bigger than the screen. All I could see was her Mary Maxim sweater with a bull moose, bigger than any moose that's ever walked the earth. I needed X-ray glasses because all I could see was the moose, but I laughed whenever Carrie laughed because I didn't want to be left out."

Next day at the mill, Wheeler said, "Skipper, I saw you at the Majestic, what did you think of the movie?" Skipper told the story about the woman with the Mary Maxim sweater with the moose like a mountain. "Probably better than the movie anyway," he said. When he was winding up with a litany of words he would have spouted to the woman if he were a little more brazen, Wheeler said, "That was my sister." Skipper reminded me, "If you're going to tell stories, you've got to know your audience."

SQUID

    no more will I
read *The Vancouver Sun*,
listen to Terry and Mary Ann,
watch Peter Mansbridge
at ten o'clock
(ten-thirty in Newfoundland)
with twenty-five million Canadians
    from Bonavista
to Vancouver Island
    from the Arctic Circle
to the Great Lake waters,
reclining in rockers
numbed with news'rotic need,
counting the final hairs
on omniscient Peter's head
in whose basset hound eyes
the world is frenetically framed:
a mess, no fit place
for human habitation,
a godforsaken
desolate wasteland

no more will I
wallow in communal muck
as I did years ago in autumn
in Roberts' Arm
watching millions
of squid throw themselves
out of the ocean,
the mass suicide
of ten-armed mollusks,
up to your knees,
the beaches of Green Bay
cream-gray with dead squid,
mustard-pumpkin rotting air,
so bad we couldn't hang
clothes outdoors or
open windows
in the October sun –
hid in our houses, stuffed
cracks with plastic bags,
to seal off manic death,
waiting for winter's relief

LUCKY DAY

I didn't win
the ten million dollar lottery,
not even a Christmas turkey,
or the office hockey pool,
and my key didn't open the car
in the centre of Lansdowne Mall.
I haven't stocked my cupboard
with a year of free Blue Ribbon tuna,
and I won't be spending Saturday
at CFCB-FM with Wailin' Wally.
After six rolls of quarters,
I still don't have a stuffed turtle
from Elliott Amusement Fair,
only my son's eyes gray with shame,
and when I peeled the plastic liner
out of the Pepsi cover
I cut my finger on the edge
and you might think
from looking at me
that I'm bitter
but I'm not
because
on the liner was a message
extraterrestrial revelation
unsolved mystery
apocalyptic epiphany

and you might think
from listening to me
that I'm bitter
but I'm not
because
hope springs like a grasshopper
like crocuses in April snow
like a dog's ears when it hears
the refrigerator door open
like a teacher's heart
when the final bell rings
and you might think
from reading me
that I'm bitter
but I'm not
because
on the plastic Pepsi liner
I read my message
in stark dark letters
like a square finger might print
in a sandy beach at twilight,
the only message I need:
TRY AGAIN

Corner Brook 1970-1989

My high school principal said,
"You ought to be a teacher."
I said, "No way." Almost two
decades faded away. I
circled back to my old school,
the principal was retired, long
gone. I was a teacher.

St. John's 1970-1976

I never wanted to be a teacher.
I wanted to be an astronomer
and watch the heavens, or
a poet and write the heavens.
I took a vocational interests inventory.
I learned I ought to be a farrier,
even though I am scared of horses.

Robert's Arm 1976-1978

Broke, I slipped into teaching.
My first year I taught grade seven
with forty-eight students.
I woke up in an alien world,
a small place where everybody
knew God's mind on everything.
I tried to fit in. I didn't fit. I left.

Toronto 1978-1979

For the big city, a world alone, where
I planned to be a pastor, but after
two months of the cemetery-like
seminary, the call passed. So I left,
sure a pastor had to be pasteurized,
when I wanted to be impure, rough,
germy, germinating.

Stephenville 1979-1985

For a little school in a town on the ocean,
a small farm perhaps, a vocation and an avocation,
where I was determined to fit in, where
I taught with fire in my eyes and heart
till the school committee called me dangerous.
I was. I left.

Fredericton 1985-1987

and left

Edmonton 1987-1989

and left

Corner Brook 1989-1990

and left

Vancouver 1990-present

Still teaching, I have turned
a circle round and round,
to know I am a teacher,
a farrier who shoes students
in order to shoo them away
with warnings to look both ways
before making left turns.

APPLE CIDER VINEGAR

As a boy, I didn't smoke in the henhouse
with Terry and Jerry, didn't play strip poker
with Jan and Jed, Holly and Pikey,
in our shed of spruce poles and cardboard
deep in the woods near the Indian steps
rising in the rock cliff to heaven
or at least to Old Man Way's house.
And that was something else I didn't do:
call the old man the Old Man.

I learned catechism for Sunday School,
tied knots for Boy Scouts,
memorized English Kings
so my brain would grow,
and when Dex said he'd replace
my broken hockey stick, I believed him.
I believed everything Dex said.

And I grew up with eyes burned blind
by darts of lightning,
innocence trapped in the scent
of garden roses, untouched thorns,
finally learned I have no talent for goodness

and wished I had stolen green apples
from Old Man Way's garden
with Terry, Jerry, Jan, Jed, Holly, Pikey, Dex,
eaten them in big bites of wild autumn cider,
expulsion from the garden inevitable
as the expiration of breath:
I can no more keep the garden
than I can swallow the moonlight.

CLIFF EDGES

I went away. Falling water imagined me
in places I have been or wish to be.
My moonlit spirit leaps off cliffs
without looking for a river to fall into.

The world is a hot, noisy place,
a pulp and paper mill.
Still the only place I want to be.
I will not write the world,

refusing to lean on light,
like Caitlin who filled binders
with scraps of disaster and dread, like
a deranged disciple of Peter Mansbridge,

well-paid to paint a world of woe,
perhaps no longer recognizing joy,
like the colour-blind, unable to
comprehend whole bands of possibility.

I will record more than the lines
of shadow's sadness leaning on light,
a rumination of rough cut stones, always
recalled in the blood's circular course.

CHARLOTTE

In our last walk to Dr. Grise's office, you sniffed
constantly, filling your senses with the full world,
a big text that you were always eager to read.

You loved Purdy's chocolate, ferreted out seasonal treats,
well hidden in closets and cupboards. You ignored
the Zeller's chocolate one pound Allan's Easter bunny.

Aaron says you could levitate, which explains
how you ate the tops of flowers in crystal vases
on high shelves, leaving the stalks intact.

Each day you invited us out of the house
to join you on a trail that never ceased to astonish,
always the sense of wonder at the unfamiliar.

I wish I had scratched your belly more, perhaps
let you kiss me with your basset hound breath,
born out of places your nose enticed you.

When you ran fast, your ears waved like a heron's wings,
and we thought you would defy gravity like a jumbo jet,
overweight with a belly that brushed the earth.

Thank you for the lessons:

Smell everything.
Run fast enough so your ears stick out straight.
Always hunger.
Forget you're a dog among other dogs.
Expect others to carry treats in their pockets.
Love children.
Take long naps.
Expect adoration.
Poop plenty.
Eat grass.
Bark, bay, howl with a heart's loud echo of each day's bounty.

FIVE TIME ZONES AWAY

I sit alone on my patio
in the late August afternoon,
a little drunk with Spring Pale Ale,
biking on the dike,
chopping wood for December fires.

I can see much of the world
through the sun and half moon
and star that hangs from my patio,
cut in iron, lined with shapes
of light and lunacy and love,

but I cannot see you, far away.
A spider's web anchors
the sun, moon, and star
to a sliver of earth where oregano,
rosemary and lemon balm grow.

Their fragrance pierces
my skin with exact jabs.
If I were a spider,
I'd cast my lines into the air
and hold the sun, moon, star

and the memory of you,
my mother. We sat on your back
porch in May-trapped sun
and talked about growing
up and older. You said,

"Learn to be happy."
I almost asked, what
is the curriculum for being
happy, but thought I would
sound too much like Doris Day.

From my patio I can almost
see you, five time zones away,
while I spin out my lines,
seeking the sun, moon and star,
the light lunacy of love in your eyes.

CINNAMON

the Coast Mountains hold
dawn like cranberry claret

a blue heron flies on raspberry light
held by the physics of air and hope

the whole sun seeps through the wings
of crows like molasses and corn syrup

the harsh light of late morning still sings
with the aftertaste of honey mustard

the noon sun in the aspens
tosses up sweet green relish

the light of early afternoon is shredded
pure orange and apricot marmalade

the holly hedge is a burst of fire
like a cinnamon heart burns the mouth

the neighbour's basset hound bays
with the breath of black bean garlic sauce

the air is sticky scarlet with memories
of words like candy apples with worms

the alders write a ragged edge of twilight
drawn with an artist's convincing precision

the late afternoon is red wine vinegar,
jalapeno jelly, and raspberry vinaigrette

in salt stung eyes, water works with fire
to remember what can't be forgotten

stories baked in a Black and Decker
bread-maker like an almond pesto loaf

served with Big Don's bread and butter
pickles and a splash of Tabasco pepper sauce

and now the full moon remembers
the day's light amidst the shadows

POETIC LICENCE

On a stone-baked autumn afternoon,
forgotten circles of seasons ago,
I backed my new Flash Gordon
red and white Chevy pick-up,
into the ditch near Uncle Jim's house.

Skipper, plum-faced with years
of yearning for a little sense,
barked, "How did you do that?"

I almost said, it wasn't hard,
I'm driving with poetic licence,
but I had enough sense to know
Skipper's question was only rhetorical,

though I was keen to offer
a television lawyer's explanation:
I don't know how to drive,
this is my first truck,
the official licence is still
on its way from St. John's,
the mirrors need adjusting,
the grass concealed the ditch,
the low sun dazzled me.

I chose a silent script instead
and before Skipper, in his disbelief,
(the most optimistic agnostic I've ever known),
could finish a fourth round of curses,
Uncle Jim strolled next door,
returned with Bud's army surplus jeep,
tied a rope to the truck and pulled it out,
saying nothing, knowing
words can't solve everything.

BARE BUFF

At the end of a busy semester, eager to avoid another day's
torrent of e-mail, I drove fast from campus and parked at Spanish Banks,
chilled by English Bay and Coast Mountain shadows,
to breathe the surprisingly clear blue sky of early December,
to stroll the beach and hold my spirit close,
the way poets need to, a brief Sabbath,
an inspiriting respite before returning to the drudge
of the associate dean's unmemorable memos
and specious spam promises of gargantuan penises.

I soon regretted my poet's fancy, wished I had stayed
with the harping safety of e-mail. A thief smashed the car
and stole my satchel: notes for essays and poems, books,
my favourite fountain pen, my diary, where for months
I had written another life, the Walter Mitty dreams,
the confused concatenation of Scorpio sun and Pisces moon,
the story behind my mask, the diary where words failed me less often,
perhaps because I wasn't writing for peer review, publication, prizes, pride.

A writer's diary, not for public presentation or perusal,
a place for gathering words like pieces of the world's puzzle,
flotsam washed up on the shore of a desert island, fragments
of an omnipresent fiction that manufactures more discontent than consent.
For months I wrote nothing, only hoped my diary was in a Smithrite,
dreamed of the thief reading it late at night by candlelight
savouring the voyeur's romance, and I waited for a dire blackmail message,
looked for its anonymous publication in *True Confessions*,
scrutinized the romantic want ads for invitations to rendezvous.

In spring, the police found my satchel on a tree stump
in Pacific Spirit Park: notes, books, fountain pen, everything
except the diary, and I woke up in Richmond Shopping Centre
on a Saturday, naked as old Adam, without fear. Now I write
only truth in my diary and poems, and expect others
will read my words with a desire for the catharsis of confession,
the revelry of revelation, the apocalypse of admission,
the dalliance of disclosure. Like Salome's head-twisting
striptease of a thousand veils, I am bare buff, but
like Lady Godiva I can still let down my hair, dreaming
the thief dreaming me, Heathcliffe on a blustery bluff.

COULEES

Not much flows in these coulees,
except the cool dry wind claiming ownership,
refusing an easy hospitality.

Shrubs, cacti, grass cling to the coulees
like a brush cut that can't hide the scalp.

Prairie grass, sage and wild rye—
no sage would try to name
all the things that grow in these coulees.

The sky is a concave ocean pulled toward the centre
of the always moving universe.

A coyote writes lines in the wind,
reminds me I cannot both see and write,
and still I write in order to see.

Like a gopher, a poet digs an intricate map
of subterranean lines with holes for popping up.

I dwell in the coulee that does not flow,
this arid coulee where cacti flame.
I see the shadows of birds but I cannot see the birds.

The sun soothes with the wind,
woos me into sleep that leaves me woozy.

I wait for the coyote and write nothing.
Perhaps writing will come
in February when I am far away,

flowing with the lines of sun and trails
and gopher hollows and the roots of cacti.

Succulents can find water where there is none,
suck the dry earth
like an orange sucks my dry mouth.

§ § §

WHISPERS

(for Anna)

Even before you were born, I talked to you
in kisses and whispers through your mother's flesh.

I was studying in a seminary at the time, still seeking
to know words, perhaps the Word that could make sense
of the March storm of questions that daily unsettled me.

From the beginning, I hoped words would keep you, though
you live quicker than I can hold the stories in my heart-memory.

I remember the little girl in a blue velvet dress,
a weekly date at the Chateau Restaurant,
when you regaled me with stories of kindergarten.

We renamed a manhole cover a womanhole cover,
perhaps the seed of your life-long feminism.

I chased the boy who destroyed the box wagon you used
for pulling dolls and almost caught him
with you bouncing in my arms, knight and princess.

You asked me to go with you to get our ears pierced,
and we went together and you hugged me.

We drove all over Vancouver for your grade 10 prom dress,
and found it, dark and grownup,
at Divine Decadence in the East End.

Just as I spoke to you in your mother's womb,
sending you soft messages of love and hope,

I speak to you in this poem to remind you that even
when you are away, wherever you are, faraway or near,
I am always calling to you

in words forged in my heart's fire for you my daughter,
filled with wonder like a field of foxglove, lupins, marigolds.

MASKS

(for Aaron)

All your life you have worn masks:
Batman Superman He-Man
the Joker the Hulk the Beast
Dracula Donatello Dick Tracy
a buxom woman, the wife of Bath

when six, you ran to Malmo Elementary
in red rubber boots, bare chest and legs,
in Edmonton's crisp autumn,
brandishing He-Man's sword,
    I have the power

my son, a thousand impersonations:
in a wig of burnt gold Phentex wool you were
Vincent the Beast and roared fearsome havoc
on Paracelsus, all enemies, all played by me

you dwell in the world of make-believe
and make me believe in worlds conjured
in words, mimetic imaginings for dispelling
each day's pressing pragmatic busyness

for years we have huddled like phantoms
in the dark of Silver City Cinemas,
shared popcorn and Pepsi, lingered long among
incarnate shadows, figures of embodied light

now, you know enough facts
about movies to win *Jeopardy*:
what three films have won all five
major categories of Academy Awards?

and you know the grammar of light,
the glamorous necromancy spelled in a tangle
of angles, shots, frames, effects, shadows

and you know how fact and fiction are
always bound in discourse, all worlds
imagined, the world's course, always in words

in a flashback, I see you flick and flicker,
down the stairs with Fred Astaire's joy,
echoes of Archimedes in Athens' streets:
I've done it, I've done it,
    I've finally written something
        I don't understand

your name starts with two a's,
in the beginning of the alphabet,
with *aardvark*, anchored in the earth:
a man of words who knows
the world well beyond words

like I always bought my father a tool
I knew he needed, like a Canadian Tire screwdriver,
you purchased a first birthday gift for me
from Shopper's Drug Mart: pencils and paper,
offered with heart language no Carlton card has inscribed:
I love having a poet for a dad
because we play with words

and not so long ago, gushing with views
about the movie we had just seen, almost
breathless, you gasped with an acrobat's grin,
I only speak thirty-three per cent of what I say,

and now I, too, have almost caught up
to my words, at least long enough to say,
I love having a poet for a son, always in play,
my words lightly resonant in this poem,
all only a fraction of all I say.

WESTERN BROOK

(for Lorna and George)

1

in the sugar-fine sands of Western Brook
my love and I baked our winter white feet,
like seed potato shoots grown in a dark cellar.
We danced in the salty sun and wind, while the trees,
wind-bent, squat, sand-blasted, clapped with joy

2

on the sand dunes,
blades of stiff grass
swept around and around
by the wind
cut like a compass,
intersecting geometric circles …
everything linked,
and my love and I
lay in the sand
and cut our shapes, too

3

the still gray-blue world rippling,
a thousand gulls calling one another,
squeaking scraping of un-oiled machinery,
calling with desire for my love and me
hidden in the sand like transparent mites
lulled by the ocean's composition,

a lion's roar, distant cannon-fire,
diastolic and systolic, speech and silence,
the silence, essential as the speech

4

my love and I danced
with tree skeletons
only shadows of trees
no longer emerald
mint lime after seasons
of snow wind sand rain
but with roots tangled
in the earth's heart
we could still hear
and dance with their song

§ § §

STONECROP

(for Vivian and Chesley)

Like stonecrop they cling to the earth
in sun-washed days and storm-lashed nights.
Together they walk the woods, seeking
tall straight trees for lumber and birch for firewood.

They hold the whole earth in their hands:
squashberry jelly with the precise measure
of tartness, a reminder where the berries come from,

bakeapple jam, every bakeapple
like a nugget of gold, gathered on endless
treks in northern peninsula bogs where
countless mosquitoes protect the treasure,

raspberries blueberries partridgeberries,
summer's fire preserved for winter's nights.
Together they have hunched over gardens
plucking weeds tangled with carrots potatoes peas.

They hold the whole earth in their hearts: trout salmon
cod rabbits caribou rhubarb cherries turnip greens,
the bounty served at family feasts for four daughters
who always return with partners bearing big appetites
and grandchildren who insist on growing taller
like grass in a wild meadow.

Together they have stood in the sun at dawn and dusk, awash
in Robinson's River, catching nothing more nor less than perspective,
they know the earth's rhythms by heart,
they know the heart turned with earth's rhythms.

WRITTEN IN THE LIGHT HEART

(for Lana)

I have never known another
so constant through seasons, decades.
We met in G. A. Mercer Junior High,
we were thirteen, joy-filled, you always laughing.

Marcus was reading the entire dictionary,
had reached D and called you and all
your girlfriends daft distaff.
I didn't know what he meant, I knew only
that I was in love with you, eager to please,
though none of you saw me.

My whole world had been Lynch's Lane
and boring facts in textbooks I had consumed
for no better reason than the promise of a prize
at the bottom like a sculpin might suck barnacles.

Years ago on Saturdays we strolled Duckworth
and Water Street, went to Woolworth's
for strawberry shortcake and milk.
At Afterwords bookstore we purchased
for a couple of dollars another armful
of books discarded from Gosling Library.
We waited for the bus outside Silver's and Sons,
dreaming of weddings and rings,
and married at twenty, ready for the world.

Except I wasn't as ready as you were.
I lived recklessly in the world, amidst
the wreckage of words, forgetting the tale
of a tower's collapse around language.

I shattered faith, was mesmerized
by the possibilities of other prepositions.
Like Silas Marner my heart was stone,
but light still found the crack.

So last summer we walked the beach
in Robinson's where we often used to
walk, where the ocean sweeps everything
into indecipherable shapes and lines,
and I took photographs for writing
faraway in winter in Steveston.

Now, July salt air blows hair across your face,
your hands are full of stones, shells, and driftwood,
while your eyes hold potent dreams,
writing always with the heart's light,
this poem also written in the light heart.

§ § §

LILACS

the clothesline is empty
but not for long,
we are home, and
Nan will hang clothes
almost every day
like semaphore flags,
signalling our presence
for the neighbours

&

the air filled with lilacs,
I walk familiar streets,
each breath I take
a long draught of childhood,
I take photographs
like storing jam preserves
for writing in winter

&

once
a seedling,
that maple tree
now more than
a story high, holds
more stories in its branches
than I have
life left
to tell

&

long ago, Pop carried
a wild rose bush
from his home in Britannia,
ancient wild rose scent
through the heart

&

summer squeezed between
the arduous winter's end,
a spring weekend or two,
and autumn's volcanic urgency,
like a slice of Maple Leaf boiled ham
that ties the tongue with traces
of cellophane and gelatine

&

in front of the house
Pop planted the snowball bush,
petals of fractal abandon, balls in balls,
like he might forget in summer
the long last winter

&

for three decades
Pop and Nan have lived
on Lomond Street, moved in
when it was new. Pop says,

“When we moved in, I could wave
to my neighbours across the gully,
but that was a long time ago, can hardly
see my neighbour’s house now,
through the lush forest,
the hidden neighbourhood,
still rooted though”

&

Pop tells me, since spring
his knees have not been good,
but in the Legion magazine he read
that cod liver oil can repair cartilage,
that he’s rebuilding his knees.
I ask him if cod liver oil can mend
a broken heart, but he says he isn’t sure,
will check the magazine later,
and I remind him about the time
he told me honey, sulphur and vinegar
could also fix any ailment, and
all he says is, “Don’t lose hope”

&

the city night lights
are embers in a campfire,
the only way I see my past,
and in my heart’s keen eye,
the clusters of houses clinging

to mountain slopes and valleys
are a meadow of wildflowers

&

this graveyard
in the middle of the city
is a tangled garden of weeds,
a forgotten place for lovers only,
a gardener's nightmare of wild rose and
chokecherry bushes, weeds, hay, forget-me-nots
and juniper berries like blood. Everything grows hot in
full cemeteries where only the headstones hint at the stories of
smallpox, house fires and drowning, mothers and children side by side
in this lost graveyard where nobody remembers
the stories of unwed mothers, criminals and the unbaptized,
buried outside the consecrated garden
of fenced plots

&

I chop wood   for winter fires
while the sun   burns my back.
My axe is too small   for one knotted log,
only nips at it with a crackie dog's spite.
I know from school mathematics
that there is a formula for dividing a circle
for finding the central   point that holds it together,
but I can't remember it   on this hot August day

&

in the midday sun on the patio, having
drunk a Black Horse or two, I forget
how to count, hear lawnmowers and
sparrows and the crash of wood trucks
on the Lewin Parkway, like a jagged
scar through the city's rock heart.
The leaves of silver asp whistle
in the breeze like light rain

&

widows and widowers
gather at Mt. Patricia Cemetery
to listen to old stories
and breathe the scent of new ones
in the plastic and silk bouquets
of grief and hope

&

never monochromatic, the sky is a dozen shades
of black and white, with a blue-light wash

&

Pop says, "She won't let me go
any further than the shed these days."
Nan says, "Not that he ever listens"

&

Nan just called out
the long-range forecast,
mostly rain for the next week

&

rain bounces off the asphalt
with the electric and geometric lines
of a pinball game

&

I just visited Pop in his shed. I wasn't sure
what he meant when he said, I'm giving
it all up soon, until he explained that
he wouldn't be making stuff
in the shed anymore

&

Nan marks each day's rhythm with food,
we eat a lot. Even before a meal is eaten
she plans the next. In fear of running out
she runs up to Dominion, though she has
enough food in the cupboard
and deep freezers to feed everybody
on Lomond Street for a year

&

Nan says,
"The toutons are right raw,"
but nobody stops eating

&

The ocean calls
on this shore forever,
for close to forever for sure.
The ocean is always changing,
a little more, a little less, always enough.
Driftwood swept in a line along the beach,
a fence around the ocean that can't be held.
The ocean always calls

&

no line will ever hold
the tangled light of beachstones,
shells, windswept trees, morning glory, and family,
beyond counting,
like fragments
in a sea arch
without end

MIST

In the solitude of sabbatical retreat
in York Harbour on the Atlantic cusp,
I am learning to hear the light of the heart
lyrically borne on titanium filaments,
strong and resilient, beyond breaking.

I live without a clock, in the heart's time,
no longer a crone's gigolo beating
to the incessant whine of chronos
measured precisely like cement blocks.

Instead of rushing from task to task,
without end or satisfaction,
I now move slowly, grounded, feel
my feet, taste the heart's rhythm.

This morning, the mountains
around York Harbour grow gray,
and leaves like orange swallows
write light on the day's dark page.

The harbour blows out to the ocean,
perhaps it will soon be a mucky basin
with up-side-down mountains,
the negative of everything I see.

The air is warm though it is almost Halloween
and the ocean churns and yearns while the wind
pushes clouds, waves, trees, until everything,
except me, is rain-washed, leaning into winter.

B. B. King sings the blues like he's watched storms
come and go, "You give me so much trouble, baby.
I don't know what to do. I ain't got nothing, ain't got
nothing now, baby, and it's all on account of you."

If I had any sense, instead of staying in a corner writing
this poem, I would bundle up in blankets and watch the storm
from the patio. But always seeking a mediated reality
I will later listen to a TV meteorologist describe the storm.

I can't render what I see, know I must
surrender to the limits of language, my words
no more than an exasperated expiration,
a hint of impossibility, things seen in a mist.

With a gasp, the storm is spent and the mountain I couldn't see
seems so close that I can reach across the harbour and touch it.
Leonard Cohen reminds me that in his writing
he blackens the page, and countless crows ride the wind.

§ § §

FIRE PIT

In the first light of winter morning,
drawn faint and tight in York Harbour,
I got up reluctantly to take the garbage out,
to face the cunning crows, hurl curses and threats,
not glad when they plunge like kamikaze pilots,
focused on the target of my Glad green garbage bags.

Last week, taking advantage of my need to pee, the crows
successfully attacked. I had to tramp out in the bitter cold
to pick up the garbage along the shoulder of the highway,
where I found scraps of poems, drafts I had scribbled,
crumpled reminders that the crows, like many editors,
were not impressed with my poems.

A little later, Lana and I, known in town as the joggers,
ran around the harbour, waved to Dave the mayor
who is always about, full of plans, laughs and stories.
We saw Glenda open the store where she bakes
old-fashioned bread and cookies. With raucous barks,
a golden Lab leaped from his yard and chased us,
clearly glad for companions on this idle morning.

I passed much of the day with poetry, others and mine,
letting words seep into my body, like night frost in morning stone.
In the late November afternoon, Lana and I cleaned out an old fire pit
we discovered in the backyard near a cliff hanging over the ocean.
We found the pit by poking around in the tall grass and tangled alders,
discovered a buried ring of rocks. Like archaeologists we conjured
images of the past, traces of people who lived here before us,

people we know nothing about, just as the people
who move in next year will know nothing
of us except in the traces we leave, will not know

that we cleared the fire pit because Aaron and Anna
and Nicholas are coming from Vancouver soon, and that
we gathered on the eve of Christmas for a wiener roast
as we have often done at faraway Garry Point
on the Gulf of Georgia,
our lives written in the rhythms of reiteration,

and while no crows have yet scrutinized these scraps scribed
in the quotidian, they are a quotient of words I leave
so others who come after us will find a bracelet of beach stones
reclaimed by Lana and me in a November afternoon, where
in late December snow-light and firelight, we roasted hot dogs
with our children, leaving hints of our presence,
the places where together we tarried a little while.

§ § §

PICNICS

(November 14, 2003)

Like an expiration date on bacon or bread, I have one more day
in my forties, and while I confess the fiction of chronology
composed by clocks and calendars, I can't dispel the relentless
realization: in a day I will be old, much older than I am now.

I will wake up on Saturday (for the first time I see weekend
as weakened) and notice how almost everyone is young,
younger than I am. Unless I am a statistical anomaly,
I will not live another fifty years, perhaps another two or three
decades, which today, with the early winter sun chasing
shadows during a long run around the curve of York Harbour,
will simply not be enough.

I don't know what eternity holds, what aftertaste of earth
will linger at the back of the heart, but I am in no hurry to find out,
since on this day I am teased to distraction with the light I see
everywhere, needing nothing more than eager licks of the earth.

Always greedy for more picnics, even as a teen
I used high school mathematics to compute the irrefutable conclusion
that eating up an annual average of fifty picnics, I would still devour
only three and a half thousand in a typical biblical lifetime, and knew
with unassailable certainty, that wouldn't be nearly enough.

Like Emily Dickinson, I know *Too few the mornings be,*
Too scant the nights, and I wonder if Emily savoured many
picnics, though probably not, since she didn't go out much, or was
that Emily Bronte? Oh the waste of getting old! After a lifetime

of rehearsing for *Jeopardy* (cramming my cheeks with facts like
a neurotic squirrel), now everything is jumbled up like jambalaya,
and all the facts are so much mouldy manna that will not sustain
me in the long winter without picnics.

And writing this poem about growing old and longing for picnics
is a sign I sing to ward off the murky monsters under my bed,
including loss and lumbago, congestion and indigestion,
headaches and heartaches, violet varicose veins like a map
of violent places I have traveled, grateful and glad Anna sent me
Walter the Farting Dog to remind me I am still loved.

PALIMPSEST

On December 7, after the balmiest
autumn ever (according to meteorologists)
winter arrived in York Harbour.

For over an hour we shovelled snow,
an aerobic workout (surprising how much
one can perspire even in frigid air).

We carved a path for *The Western Star*
(urgent daily news) and tramped to the cliff
to see the winter sea.

Today our path is still a jagged serpentine
scratch in the backyard snow
like a sheet of vellum.

Soon more snow will come and erase
the line we wrote yesterday,
but we'll clear more paths

like drafts of writing,
impermanent, transitory traces,
both visible and invisible.

The backyard is a text scribbled
by fluted flux, flowing beyond bounds
of language and literacy,

writing in the moment, an eternal present
like a palimpsest, nothing ever lost,
even if no longer legible.

CRANBERRIES

Snow falls in York Harbour. There is light everywhere,
except in the jade harbour, in the granite scars slashed
in the circle of mountains where nothing can cling.

This morning, Lana and I stripped the Christmas tree,
hauled it to the cliff as an offering for the creatures
who lived here a long time before us and will a long time after us.

Crows convene for the feast of cranberries and popcorn
we strung a few weeks ago, before the children flew
across the country to check out our sabbatical solitude.

For a couple of decades at least and in at least five provinces,
we have strung cranberries and popcorn, memories
for recounting like garnet beads on an abacus.

This fragile line of cotton can't be broken, holds fast
to family feasts, treats for crows, more memories
than any dictionary or even the alphabet can store.

We played Trivial Pursuit, Cranium, Scrabble and cards,
hearts usually seemed to be trumps,
and we watched Arnold Schwarzenegger films.

We gathered for Chinese food on Christmas Eve,
Christmas morning brunch in York Harbour,
Christmas dinner for twenty at Nan and Pop's.

Squeezed in the Honda, we swung along the shore
through Frenchman's Cove, Benoit's Cove, Halfway
Point, Mt. Moriah to Corner Brook and back many times.

We celebrated Ella's christening, Sam and Claire's wedding,
Lana and Lorna's fiftieth birthday, Anna's plans, New Year's Eve
with Newfie Duck and Dollar Store sparklers.

Aaron, Nick, and I drank only Newfoundland beer
(India Pale Ale, Black Horse, Dominion, Blue Star,
Jockey Club) even if it tasted just like Canadian beer.

We shot pool at the Summit, ate fries with ground beef,
gravy, and onions, Mary Brown's taters, pizza at Sorrento's
and went to the Majestic to see Russell Crowe fight Napoleon.

The children made angels in the snow, resurrected Frosty,
slid down the backyard hill on an old toboggan they had left
in Pop's shed more than a dozen years ago.

They left yesterday, and now like a crow I will eat cranberries
and recount how we gathered this one Christmas
on the other coast with long breaths of Atlantic salt air.

We will never gather in York Harbour again, in this place
where we are all visitors in a song sung once only to the moon
tugged sea, in this singular chapter that simply can't be iterated.

Snow, winter night moonlight caught in birch branches
like thin fingers scratched in supplication in the charcoal sky,
all traces long erased, even before we leave.

FORGET-ME-NOTS

(for Lana, February 14, 2006)

Long ago and faraway, on a July morning
chilly with North Atlantic gusts,
we ran along the shore of the Humber Arm
on the gravel shoulder of the harbour arterial.
Giant trucks boomed their loads
of spruce and fir logs to the mill,
blew our caps off, left us scrambling in a wreckage
of words tossed in the wind

and you asked, as you sometimes do,
sometimes persist, why did you return?

The question clung in the air,
still, after so many years,
like light blue forget-me-nots clinging
in the crevices of the rock and gravel gully
off the highway's edge, like a faint memory
of a meadow, wildflowers beyond counting.

But this poem is no bunch of forget-me-nots
grabbed from the gully in a frantic effort
to appease you for my forgetting
too many Valentine's Days and love's just hopes.

I returned (at best, any explanation
will be an agnostic's confession, tangled in a network
of lines and tight knots that can't be traced,
a rhizome with no beginning, no closure)
like a salmon, compelled by a heart memory
of home and hope alone, knowing how I would never
write a new poem without you.

Siren-like, I was seduced by my own fictions,
mesmerized by my own myths, another Othello obsessed
with his storied image in Desdemona's eyes …
ordinary exploits rendered extraordinary in the rapt telling,
Desdemona swooning until old Othello
saw only an O in her heart through which he aimed
to jump to unknown places he had to know,
a last frontier irresistible to his imagination.

True love is the story of long love, not lost love.
C.S. Lewis (who knew more about love than most)
told Sheldon Vanauken that love always dies
and even your wife's death is a severe mercy
since now your love will never die,
hogwash Lewis couldn't believe a few years later
as his own wife lay dying.

We weave the warp and weft of words and lines
like threads, attentive in the small rhythms
of each day's seamless simplicity, knowing in our blood,
tensions and directions that render a sturdy lace
that provides tender warmth in a North Atlantic storm,

like a Valentine's Day bouquet
    of forget-you-nots,
        steeped in love's light.

§ § §

TRACES

Three gulls, gray and white, gasp
in a gust of winter wind.

On the hill next door,
spruce trees like stoic giants
guard the deserted house.

The day is a Gerry Squires lithograph,
lines of light etched lightly.

In this place where we dwell for a year
before resuming our old lives,
we leave a swathe pressed by snowshoes,

but our tracks fill up almost as fast
as we walk, leaving few traces

as the gulls write a long story
with the quills of their wings
filled with India ink and hoarfrost.

MAD DOG POND

Yesterday, we snow-shoed a trail that winds
over a marsh through tuckamore to Mad Dog Pond
hidden in a mountain valley. We passed the remnants
of an ancient forest fire in air so still and cold
we had no breath for talking,

amid alders and birch, tall, spare, spindly,
like Alex Colville's elderly, naked self-portrait,
while spruce and fir trees wore snow like ermine
wraps on the shoulders of Chekhov's dowagers.

Today, dollops of snow cling to windows
like miniature starfish and in the backyard I can
still see the wyes of birds' feet and geometric circles
drawn by a cat, a rabbit or my imagination.

Suspended in Northeast gusts, seagulls are
attached to the sky by filaments of hope.
Snow slowly sweeps into waves, rises
like sea spray, flecks of steel in the wind.

The world rendered unfamiliar hides
honed edges, creates a realm of curves, undulations,
and round echoes like Elizabeth Arden's make-up
conceals crevices, gaps, stark lines

and Farley Mowat is wrong, once again, since
the Inuit do not have a voluminous vocabulary
for snow (Franz Boas was misinterpreted,
exotic fiction being more entertaining than fact).

Only a poet, with a compulsion for control,
would try to embrace snow in the alphabet, an impossible task
since snow can't be named or tamed in words any more
than I can shovel the snow in my backyard back to the sky.

§ § §

ETCH-A-SKETCH

On a blustery day in late January, we snow-shoed
from our side door through the backyard of a neighbour
who moved to Fort MacMurray long ago. We wrote
a trail through the woods to the beach, following the traces
of snowmobiles along the jagged edge of the frozen sea.

We could see the houses of York Harbour, the cottages
on Wood's Island, a hint of the Gulf of St. Lawrence and
Wee Ball and other islands whose names we had yet to learn.
Gulls hung in the air hoping we had food or perhaps were food.

Lana said, *do you think we could stay here, forever?*
I couldn't hear her question, occupied with the way snow, like
an Etch-a-Sketch, obliterates the lines and permutations
of past images. Like Jesus walked on the Sea of Galilee,

suspended on snowshoes I defy the laws of physics
and walk across a plain of snow, almost forgetting
the marsh muck below my feet, focused only on the lightness
of snow, walking in a world draped for a wedding feast.

SPRING

April 21, 2004

1

Spring almost consumes York Harbour
and the winter scribed mountains
in eccentric moments of light etched stories.
But most of the time, spring creeps into town
with a cat's process of fits and starts, interruptions,
surprises and glimpses of blue sky and sunlight,
followed by a sudden snowfall and a gust of wind
that knocks you off your feet, taking your breath away.

2

Every few minutes the vibrations of the sump pump
shake the cottage. Confident that no memory of winter
will flood the basement, its vibrations are a chorus,
as spring gurgles, creeks and swirls,
to our final gasp of relief that *spring is here,*
until an easterly wind blows in the harbour
with enough ice to drive you back indoors:
some cold, I'll crank up the thermostat.

3

The men of York Harbour stand firmly astride
mountains of ploughed snow and ice, like an
iceberg fell from the sky into their front yards.
Helping Mother Nature, they hack and chop
winter's legacy, dump the snow into Main Street,
afraid if they don't, the snow will be there in July,
a boorish guest who won't go home. Like Hillary
and Tenzing Norgay, they stand victorious on the peaks
of mountains, but they are seeking no Everest
conquest, just a path to the grass and dandelions
they fondly remember mowing months ago.

4

Yesterday, Lana found a violet crocus
in the front yard. With a brazen orange
pistil, gaudier than a San Diego bird
of paradise, it poked through the decayed
grass and faded brown earth. I danced
a welcome. Today the radio deejay predicts
twenty-five centimeters of snow, erratic spring tease.

CROSS-WORD PUZZLE

(York Harbour, May 13, 2004)

In this sacred place of solitude on the edge
of the North Atlantic we live each day with sturdy
rhythms and hold one another in the heart's light.

Yesterday, you raked autumn hay in the backyard,
while I took a respite from revisions to an essay,
and watched you a long time through the patio door.

On this the fourth anniversary since we married again,
adding another surprise twist to our story,
sewn with jagged and joyful seams, we are here.

We wear two wedding bands, the past and more past,
reaching into the eager present and future,
nothing forgotten, everything stored and restored.

We have turned a circle of seasons, and though
we will never leave this place, we know, also, that
we will never return, since all turns are new.

Today, we biked four hours on a trail built for caribou
and ATV's, a scribbled loop of mud paths that our legs
couldn't hold. You took more risks than me,

shot down somersaulting hills, paused to photograph
my descent, laughed with my chasing you over shards
of rock, washouts, jagged ruts in a marsh of tangled roots.

Our stories intersect like words in a crossword puzzle,
letters shared, vertical and horizontal lines woven into
a quilt of many colours, to keep us through every season.

We stopped at Sheppard's Grocery in Lark Harbour
to buy champagne, and tonight we will celebrate our
long lasting love, while watching *Survivor.*

LIGHT LINES

(for Rita)

With winter's end, silver birches stand
along the parallel borders of the highway,
bare and lean, awash in late afternoon light,
a topsy-turvy sea of vertical waves,
iterable far beyond the keenest eyesight.

Like Charlton Heston commanded the parting
of the Red Sea in Cecil B. DeMille's dazzling
miracle, the highway is a charcoal line
that divides and defines the tangled wilderness
in a text that invites and defies perspective.

The birches hold light like Chinese lanterns.
I want to learn how to breathe light,
to hold its scent long in memory, to hear
light seep into stone, to taste savoury light
on the skin and to know the language of light.

Like I once stood in a Richmond gallery
surrounded by Rita's art, her imagined trees
and light rendered with heart and hand,
I now linger again, face to face
with the limits of language, and wonder

how Rita would evoke the silver birches
full of spring light, and I wish for the artist's
sense of knowing, want to write the lines
of light I have witnessed, so you can know
how light dances up a storm beyond words.

BEACHSTONES

to see what is really there and to record it
as it is—without dramatizing or striving for effect
(D.R. Cowles, Canadian photographer)

&

In the Wiseman's house
at the end of Main Street
in York Harbour, faraway
on the North Atlantic's edge,
I am slowly learning how
to live sabbatically,
drawing silence
like the sun calls the sea.

&

Winter hasn't yet arrived
in York Harbour where
autumn has been a long
weekend without end,
but I'm sure snow will soon come
with poems like spiced apple cider.

&

In the boreal forest that clings
to the Long Range Mountains
the trees have been named
with simple descriptors:
black spruce, white pine, black ash,
white birch, red maple, yellow birch,

but someone with a poet's eye
named one tree *trembling aspen*,
the only tree I can identify.

&

Winter arrived today
wrapped in windy whispers,
enough to stop the heart
in the circle of long months,
and the harbour seems smaller,
with snow, mist and low clouds
in the mountains and sea
like winter shrinks everything.

&

While I revised this poem
the oil furnace stopped blowing.
Sam, the Irving's repairman,
is on his way. I hope he arrives soon
because on this winter's day,
I am Bob Cratchit, scratching figures
in Ebenezer Scrooge's accounts.
I don't want to whine, but this poem
is failing to keep us warm.

&

In the tangled midst of memories,
the resilient heart calls out
for a poet's language with the breath

of moist rum-soaked fruit cake
like Lana just made for Christmas.

&

Silence falls like March snow,
full of surprises seen in the window.

&

After hauling lobster traps near
Little Port Head, fishermen return
in a pumpkin orange dory with green
gunwales. A flume of spray stretches
out like the tail of a kite. Seagulls chase
the boat, calling out raucously for scraps
the fishermen might leave.

&

The dandelions close up
at night and in rain,
then spring open
yellow hearts in the sun.

&

I want to stand naked
in the spring rain
    and
grow like daffodils
open to language.

&

June 21,
the first day of summer,
fog and rain, capelin weather.
Wore gloves while out walking.
Turned the thermostat up.
No sign of summer.

&

In this place, the sun rises
in the harbour and light
and shadow are the alphabet
that composes the senses
and poems for sustaining
stillness and stability.

&

Like the countless beachstones
that line York Harbour,
I can't tell you the stories
I have lived in this place,
clutching the wild
chaotic world in my words.

§ § §

Versions of some of these poems have been published in the following journals:

Grain, The Fiddlehead, Prairie Journal of Canadian Literature, TickleAce, Event, Green's Magazine, JCT: Journal of Curriculum Theorizing, Canadian Stories, Toasted Cheese, stonestone, Educational Insights, Poetry WLU, arts-informed, New Canadian Review.

ACKNOWLEDGEMENTS

In addition to recognizing my wife Lana, her parents, and her sisters in the book's dedication, I also wish to acknowledge an extended group of supportive family and friends. First, for inspiring the poems I thank my children, Anna and Aaron, who live always in the light of words and imagination. Also, I thank my parents, Russell (Bud) and Kerry Leggo, who tell me their stories and never complain about my translations. I am always grateful to my brother, Rick Leggo, and my sister, Wanda Legge, for being glad their brother grew up to be a poet. In addition, I am thankful for family connections that include my children's partners, Nicholas Reithmeier and Penny Adam, and a network of in-laws, nephews, and nieces, bearing the surnames Gillingham, Sweetapple, and Goudie, especially George, Doug, and Craig, who all know how to play 120's and laugh a lot. Moreover, for encouraging me to live creatively, I offer hearty thanks to my wise and energetic colleagues: Rita Irwin, Karen Meyer, Lynn Fels, Norm Amundson, Erika Hasebe-Ludt, Joe Belanger, Peter Gouzouasis, Kit Grauer, George McWhirter, and Ted Aoki. Also, I thank Rebecca Rose for her generous support, and Tom Henihan for his careful and thoughtful editing.

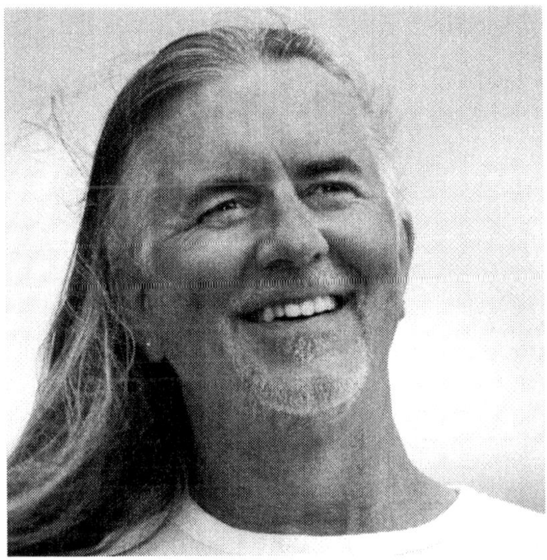

CARL LEGGO
Photography: Bruce McCaughey